A HORRID HENRY BOOK

HORRID HENRY'S
GHOSTS

Francesca Simon spent her childhood on the beach in California, and then went to Yale and Oxford Universities to study medieval history and literature. She now lives in London with her family. She has written over fifty books and won the Children's Book of the Year in 2008 at the Galaxy British Book Awards for *Horrid Henry and the Abominable Snowman*.

Tony Ross is one of Britain's best-known illustrators, with many picture books to his name as well as line drawings for many fiction titles. He lives in Wales.

For a complete list of
Horrid Henry titles, visit

www.horridhenry.co.uk

or

www.orionbooks.co.uk

A HORRID FACTBOOK

HORRID HENRY'S
GHOSTS

Francesca Simon
Illustrated by Tony Ross

Orion
Children's Books

First published in Great Britain in 2014
by Orion Children's Books
a division of the Orion Publishing Group Ltd
Orion House
5 Upper Saint Martin's Lane
London WC2H 9EA
An Hachette UK company

1 3 5 7 9 10 8 6 4 2

Text © Francesca Simon 2014
Illustrations © Tony Ross 2014

The moral right of Francesca Simon and Tony Ross to be identified
as author and illustrator of this work has been asserted.

Facts compiled by Sally Byford.

ISBN 978 1 4440 1152 4

A catalogue record for this book is available from the British Library.

Printed in Great Britain by
Clays Ltd, St Ives plc

www.orionbooks.co.uk

www.horridhenry.co.uk

CONTENTS

Hello from Henry

Helloooooooo Gang! Helloooooooo
ghosthunters! BAH! Who's scared of
ghosts? Certainly not me. (As long as
they aren't giant bunnies or carrying
needles or looking like Miss Battle-Axe
or howling or...)

Well, as I was saying, it takes a lot
more than some old spook to spook me!
That's why I've had such fun collecting
these spine-tingling stories about
haunted houses and things that go bump
in the night.

But I'm not scared. Ha! Who, me? Fearless leader of the Purple Hand Gang? Are you joking?

Hang on. What was that banging noise? Were those footsteps on the stairs? Did I hear chains rattling? And that horrible howling...shhh...can you hear it?

Woooooooooooooooooooooooo.

Ha Ha scared you!! Tee hee. Happy haunting!

Henry

GHOSTLY
FIRST FACTS

You've seen ghosts at the movies and scared your friends with **spooky** stories – but how much do you **really** know about them?

Ghosts are thought to be the spirits of people who have **died**, returning to haunt the places they've left behind. But **why** do spirits come back as ghosts? There are a few different theories:

It's often believed that ghosts return to **communicate** with the living – either to **warn** family or friends of danger, or to take **revenge**.

Some think that people who die in a **horrible** way return to experience their final hours **over and over** again. Some ghosts might not even **know** they are dead – that's why they carry on as if they are **still alive**.

What's certain is that people have been **fascinated** by ghosts since **ancient times**. The **first ghost story** ever recorded is by the Roman author, Pliny the Younger. He wrote about a house that was being haunted by the ghost of an old man with **clanking chains** around his wrists and legs.

Today, around **10%** of people believe they have **seen a ghost** of one sort or another. They describe misty images, moving columns of cold air, or **spooky sounds and smells**.

And as many as **50%** of people believe that ghosts exist – even if they've **never seen one**.

Of course, lots of people **don't believe** in ghosts – they say the sightings are just imagined, and demand **real proof**.

But since ghostly activities are **paranormal**, which means they don't follow the rules of science or nature, how can they be proved?

Do **YOU** believe in ghosts? Read on . . . if you **dare** . . .

SPOOK
SPOTTING

Some people are willing to brave the **spookiest** of places in search of ghosts. They are called **ghost hunters**.

Could YOUR house be **haunted**? There are certain **clues** that every ghost hunter knows to look out for . . .

Do you ever hear **unexplained** noises –
like footsteps, knocking, or strange bangs
and tapping? Maybe your house is just **old
and creaky**, but maybe, just maybe, it's
something more.

Have you ever found your bedroom light **on**
when you're sure you switched it **off**, or a
door slammed **shut** when you know you left
it **open**? It could be the work of a **ghost**.

Do your batteries **mysteriously** run out? Ghost hunters think that ghosts need **energy sources** to appear. If electrical equipment is **draining** very quickly, it could mean there's a ghost about.

Does your cat ever seem to **stare** at something you can't see? Animals have **sharper senses** than humans and paranormal researchers think they may be more sensitive to **ghostly activity**.

Have you ever felt the **hairs** on the back of your neck **stand up**, or suddenly felt all **cold** and **shivery**? Have you had that strange, **creepy** feeling you're being **watched**? There might be a **ghost** nearby . . .

Of course **real ghost hunters** can't rely on a general 'feeling'. Their job is to try and prove that ghosts exist using **scientific** methods. They rely on **high-tech gadgets** to pick up temperature changes and unusual energy in the air.

Ghost hunters also look out for a smelly **ghostly goo** called **ectoplasm**, which looks a bit like egg whites, that ghosts are said to leave behind them.
Blecccch!

The stars of American TV series **'Ghost Hunters'** have been searching for ghosts for **20 years**. They haven't seen one yet, but they keep looking . . .

And ex-Blue Peter presenter Yvette Fielding and her husband hunted for ghosts over **14 seasons** of the British TV series **'Most Haunted'**, but **never** managed to capture a single spook on camera.

If you fancy your chances as a ghost hunter, why not visit the **Mermaid Hotel in Rye**? It claims to have ghosts in four of its rooms. One guest said she awoke in the night to see two ghosts fighting a **duel!**

You'll get an **award** if you last a whole night at the **Haunted Vicarage in Sweden**. One visitor claimed to have woken to see the ghosts of **three old women** staring at her. They didn't even disappear when she turned the light on!

Why not try a **ghost tour** somewhere really spooky, like **Pluckley village in Kent**, said to be the **most haunted** village in England? Visit the **Screaming Woods** and **Fright Corner** and you might catch some ghostly glimpses.

There's the **Screaming Man**, who was trapped in a wall of clay, the Highwayman, who was **stabbed** by villagers, or the Watercress Woman, who set herself **alight** by accident while drinking gin.

CREEPY CASTLES AND HAUNTED HOUSES

Castle ruins and big old houses are perfect places for **spook-spotting.** Nearly all of them claim to have ghosts **haunting** the halls or **floating** along the corridors.

Windsor Castle is said to be haunted by the ghost of **Queen Elizabeth I**. Her footsteps have been heard in the library and she has been seen walking the walls. Her body is buried at Westminster Abbey, but it's thought she returns to Windsor to **check on** the current king or queen!

For over 900 years, ghostly goings-on have been reported at the **Tower of London** – like the Countess of Salisbury, who in 1541 ran screaming from her execution block followed by the axe man, and now replays her **bungled beheading** on the anniversary of her death.

Rochester Castle in **Kent** is haunted by Lady Blanche de Warren, who has an **arrow** still stuck in her chest. Her husband-to-be **shot** her by mistake at **Easter 1264**. Ouch.

Then there are the two young princes in the Tower of London, who are said to have been **murdered** by their uncle, King Richard III, and now appear hand-in-hand in their nightgowns. Guy Fawkes' **spine-tingling screams** have also been heard echoing through the Tower as though he is still being **tortured**.

At the **Buma Inn** in **Beijing**, China, the ghost of a guest **poisoned** by the hotel chef walks the corridors, **hunting** for his killer – who **stabbed** himself before he could be brought to justice!

Bramshill House in **Hampshire** tells of the legend of the **Mistletoe Bride** – a young woman who accidentally **suffocated** in a chest during a game of hide-and-seek one Christmas. Her hiding place was **so good** that no one found her. Now she is said to wander the house looking for someone to release her.

Bisham Abbey in **Berkshire** is haunted by the ghost of **Lady Hoby**, who weeps and washes her **bloodstained** hands. She locked her son William in a cupboard as a **punishment**, then left for London, forgetting to tell anyone where he was. By the time he was found, it was **too late**.

Fort George in Novia Scotia is Canada's most haunted historic site. Visitors have reported seeing the ghost of a little girl following tour groups, and people have felt her **holding their hands**.

Okiku's Well in Himeji Castle, Japan, is said to be haunted. The story goes that the castle's owner was in love with Okiku, a beautiful servant, but she did not love him in return. Angry, he tricked her into believing she had lost one of the family's ten precious plates, then **threw her down the well**. Now, at night, she rises, and counts the plates out loud. When she reaches nine, she **screams** and returns to the well.

WHO'S WHOOO?

Supernatural stories have been told all over the world for thousands of years. Check out these **ghosts from around the globe**.

In the **UK**, you might spot a misty **White Lady** haunting old castles or lonely country lanes. They are said to be women who suffered **tragic deaths** before ending up as **gloomy ghosts**.

Strigoi are the ghosts of people who have died unhappily in **Romania**. They have bright red hair and bluish-purple eyes, and they **drink human blood**.

Road ghosts are often reported in the **UK** and **America**. Most famous is the legend of **Mary**. Killed on her way home from a party in **Chicago**, USA, she waits at the side of the road at night. Drivers who pick her up only realise it's her when she suddenly shouts **"Stop here!"** at the graveyard and **disappears**.

In **Ireland**, noisy spirits called **banshees** are said to have a **scream** so loud it can **shatter glass**. If you hear one, you will **die** a violent death within a year.

25

Zashiki-warashi are ghosts of **Japanese** children. They are believed to cause all sorts of **mischief**, like pinching your pillow while you sleep, or pulling your hair. But they can change in a flash into a dark, scary **beast** that crawls along the floor.

The terrifying **Indonesian toyol** is a tiny **green-skinned goblin** ghost with glowing red eyes. Don't let them near your feet – they love **drinking blood** from people's toes.

In **Scandinavia**, stories of the **gjenganger** are enough to give you nightmares. If one pinches you, your skin will turn **blue** and you'll **die**.

Skondhokatas from **India** are ghosts of people who have **lost their heads** in train accidents. They can be spotted standing alone at night in train stations. They are said to be **violent**, so approach at your peril!

The **Russian domovoy** looks like a tiny old man with a furry face. He helps around the house and **tickles** people when they're asleep. He likes things to be clean and tidy, and he'll **hurt** lazybones who don't clean their homes.

In **China**, people believe that the wicked return as **hungry ghosts**, with big, fat bellies and long, thin necks. If they aren't left **mountains of food**, they will go after the living . . .

PESKY POLTERGEISTS

Poltergeists can't be seen, but they are probably the **best-known** and **most feared** type of ghost. They are **spiteful** spirits – instead of haunting a place, they pick on a particular **person** to torment.

The first record of a poltergeist is from **Germany** in **856** AD, when it was reported that a noisy ghost **threw stones** at a family and **started fires** at their farmhouse. 'Poltergeist' is, in fact, a German word meaning 'noisy ghost', so this may be when the name was first used.

In many poltergeist hauntings, people report strange **noises** and knockings, and objects **moving about by themselves**.

But sometimes hauntings are more **serious**. Strange marks appear on walls or furniture, or **mysterious scratches** on a person's skin. And in rare cases, poltergeists can get really **nasty** – starting **fires** or **hitting** someone.

In **Connecticut**, USA, in **1850**, the Phelps family returned home from church to find their doors open wide, cutlery and books flying around, and pillows and sheets fluttering in the air. During the following weeks, their daughter was **slapped** by something unseen, and their son was lifted into the air and **thrown into water**. No one could explain these **weird** happenings.

In **1658**, in **Northamptonshire**, the Stiff family claimed **strange things** were happening in their house – shoes floated about, a loaf of bread **danced** around the kitchen, and on one occasion everyone watched in horror as a **carving knife** hurtled towards a servant point-first, Luckily, at the last minute it hit him with the handle instead.

One night in **Texas**, USA, in the **1960s**, a man called Mr Baeird and his son were **terrorised by bugs**. Dead bugs and **slimy slugs** appeared from nowhere around their house. Some people blamed a poltergeist, but others said it was probably just an angry Mrs Baeird!

At the **Victoria Palace Theatre** in **London**, staff say they often find **wigs** flying around the wig room. Witnesses describe it as a '**hair-raising** experience'.

Greyfriars Cemetery in **Edinburgh** is said to be haunted by the Mackenzie Poltergeist, named after an **evil** man, George Mackenzie, who is buried there. Visitors have reported being **cut** and **bruised** by something invisible, and have even been **knocked unconscious**!

The **Enfield Poltergeist** became well-known in the **1970s**. The activity revolved mainly around the two girls of the house – Margaret, 12, and Janet, 11 – who were even captured on camera supposedly **levitating** in their bedroom.

In **Bavaria**, in the **1960s**, when a lawyer's office was troubled by heavy furniture **moving on its own**, people said it was a poltergeist. But when a young woman who worked there left, the weird events stopped. Did the poltergeist just **follow** her to her next job?

ARMY
APPARITIONS

There are always **spooky stories** about **old battle sites** – and paranormal researchers believe that's because the **violence** of battle leaves a kind of 'ghostly recording' on the landscape.

They also think that sometimes soldiers die so suddenly that their ghosts just **carry on fighting** . . .

On 23rd October **1642**, thousands of soldiers died in the terrible **Battle of Edgehill**. In the following weeks, people reported seeing **phantom soldiers** in the night sky above Edgehill, fighting the battle **all over again**.

At the **Alamo** church in **Texas**, USA, nearly 200 Texan defenders were **slaughtered** by the Mexican army after a 13-day siege in **1836**. When Mexican troops returned later to **demolish** the church, six ghostly soldiers chased them away waving **flaming swords**.

At the **Battle of Mons** during the **First World War**, the British army was losing to the Germans . . . until **thousands** of **phantom bowmen**, said to be from the Battle of Agincourt in **1415**, suddenly appeared. The German horses turned and fled.

The **USS Lexington**, an aircraft carrier from the **Second World War**, is now a floating museum in **Texas**, USA. Over 200 visitors say they have been offered a tour of the Engine Room by a young sailor – it's only later they realise they've met Charlie, the ghost of the engine room operator who was **killed** on duty when a Japanese torpedo struck the ship in **1943**.

When archaeologists discovered a **Roman road** buried under the **Treasurer's House in York**, a tale told years before suddenly started to make sense. In **1953**, a plumber claimed he had seen **ghostly Roman soldiers** marching across the cellar – but only from their **knees** upwards!

No one has ever identified the **Unknown Warrior**, a soldier killed in action and brought back from France in **1920** to be buried in **Westminster Abbey**, London. But he must still be remembered by the ghost of another First World War soldier, who it's said often appears before the grave, stands for a few minutes with his head bowed in respect, and then **slowly disappears**.

BEASTLY
HAUNTINGS

It isn't just humans who are thought to return as ghosts. **Animal ghosts** seem to return for much the same reasons as humans – to **haunt** the place they died, to **comfort** a much-loved owner, or for **revenge**.

In **1816**, a soldier at the **Tower of London** reported being attacked by a **gigantic bear**. He fought back, but his weapon passed straight through the bear. The animal was thought to be a ghost from **200 years earlier** when there was a **zoo** in the tower.

In the **1700s**, a gang of men entered the Anchor Tavern in London to force men to join the King's Navy. A dog tried to protect his master, but the gang slammed a door on the dog, cutting off its tail. They say the ghost dog is still often sighted, as the pub closes, **searching for its tail**.

In **Wales**, near Colyne Bay, a man was driving along the road when a **large white horse** suddenly leaped over a hedge in front of his windscreen. **Terrified**, the man slammed on his brakes – but the horse was **nowhere** to be seen.

At **King John's Hunting Lodge** in Axebridge, Somerset, sightings of the ghost of a **friendly tabby cat** have often been reported. The cat enters a room through a closed door and curls up on the floor before **disappearing**.

A **Great Dane** called Kabar, belonging to film star Rudolph Valentino, died in **1929** and was buried in the **Los Angeles Pet Cemetery** in California. Visitors to Kabar's famous grave often claim that they have seen him, and he has even given them a **big slobbery lick**!

But not all animal ghosts are friendly – the **Black Dog** is a **fearsome phantom** in the form of a huge black dog with eyes like **glowing red coals,** which brings **bad luck** to anyone who sees it.

In the **seventeenth century**, a Black Dog ghost haunted **Peel Castle** on the **Isle of Man**. It would lie by the fire in the guards' room every night. All the guards refused to walk around the castle alone – until one man decided to risk it. As he set off, the dog **followed** him. Shortly after, the guard's **screams** echoed around the castle. He **never spoke again** and **died** three days later.

Another headless Black Dog is said to haunt **Ivelet Bridge** in **Yorkshire**. The dog **leaps** over the side of the bridge and into the water. According to reports, anyone who sees it **dies** within a year. The last sighting was around a hundred years ago . . . or was it?

TOP TEN: FAMOUS PHANTOMS

Some ghost stories are told time and time again. Here are **ten top tales of terror**.

The ghost of famous eighteenth century highwayman **Dick Turpin** has been spotted all over England. He gallops along **unlit** roads on his horse, Black Bess, and **preys** on people at **lonely** crossroads.

2 **Al Capone** was the best-known **gangster** in America in the early twentieth century. Imprisoned on **Alcatraz Island** in San Francisco, he learned to play the banjo. Though he was released to die at home, prison warders still claimed to hear his **ghostly songs** long after his death.

3 The **Flying Dutchman** is a legendary **ghost ship**. In **1641**, a Dutch ship **sank** off the coast of Africa. The captain screamed a **curse** – that he would finish his journey even if he had to keep sailing till the **end of time**. It's now said that whoever sees the ship will die a terrible death.

4 In **1974** a family of six were **murdered** in their home in **Amityville**, USA. When a new family moved into the house, they were terrorised by noise, **green slime** and ghost sightings, and moved out within a month. Between 1979 and 2013, 11 films were released based on the story.

5 The **Man in Grey** is one of **London's** best-known ghosts. He haunts the **Theatre Royal** in Drury Lane. He is said to be the spirit of a wealthy man from the eighteenth century, who was in **love** with one of the actresses and who was **brutally murdered** by a jealous rival.

In **1817**, the Bell family from **Tennessee**, USA, claimed they were tormented by a poltergeist who became known as the **Bell Witch**. It began with bed covers being pulled off at night. Then things got really scary. The youngest daughter, Betsy, complained that an **invisible** being would **pull her hair** and **slap** her, leaving **handprints** on her face and body. The poltergeist continued to **torment** the Bell family until the death of the father, John Bell, in 1820.

7 The **Island of the Dolls**, near **Mexico**, is haunted by the spirit of a little girl who **drowned** on the island. A local man turned the island into a **shrine** by hanging **dolls** by the **hundreds** in trees. Visitors say they've seen the dolls move, beckon and even **speak** to them. Spooky!

8 According to folklore, **Bloody Mary** is the ghost of Mary Worth, killed for being a **witch**. It's said that if you go **alone** into a darkened room, sit in front of a mirror and shout her name **three times**, Mary's face will appear.

9 The headless ghost of **Queen Anne Boleyn** is frequently sighted at the **Tower of London**, carrying her head tucked underneath her arm. The second wife of Henry VIII of England, Anne was **imprisoned** in the Tower of London in **1536** for **witchcraft** and publicly **executed**.

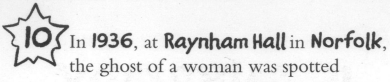

10 In **1936**, at **Raynham Hall** in **Norfolk**, the ghost of a woman was spotted coming down a large staircase, wearing a brown dress and with **empty holes** for eyes. It's been said she **haunts** the hall because her husband locked her up and never let her leave. Two photographers snapped her ghost, and their photo of the **Brown Lady** became famous.

IS ANYBODY THERE?

In the **mid-nineteenth century**, a group
of people called **Spiritualists** believed it was
possible to **talk to ghosts**. They came together
to try and **contact the dead** in meetings
called séances, and this still happens today.

Séances are usually led by a person called
a **medium**, who claims they can **hear the
voices** of the dead.

Early mediums used '**table turning**' or 'tapping'
to communicate with ghosts. The medium
would call out letters of the alphabet, and the
table would knock on the floor in response,
slowly forming a **message** from the spirit.

Other mediums used **spirit writing**. A small basket was attached to a pencil, the ghost entered the basket and **guided** the medium's hand to write a message.

Table tapping was slow and spirit writing often hard to read, so by the **late 1800s** a **new** way to communicate with the dead was invented: the **Ouija** (or talking) board.

Players of the Ouija board rest their fingers on a pointer, and the ghost moves it to letters and numbers on the board to **spell a message**.

The Ouija board was originally sold as **a toy** – it outsold Monopoly in 1966. Its **spooky** advertising slogan was: "**It's only a game – isn't it?**" But paranormal researchers have always **warned** people not to play with the Ouija board, saying that **evil spirits** could be contacted by mistake.

In **1999**, it was good news for Iris Maloney when she won **$1.4 million** in the **California** lottery. She **thanked her Ouija board**, which she claimed had helped her pick the winning numbers.

In **1920**, police in the town of El Cerrito, **USA**, arrested seven people who had become **hysterical** after using a Ouija board. But the 'Ouijamania' spread, and when one of the police officers **stripped** off his clothes and ran into the bank **naked**, officials **banned** Ouija boards from the town.

In **1933**, in the **USA**, Mattie Turley **shot** and **killed** her father after playing the Ouija board with her mother. She claimed in court that **the board had told her to do it**.

The *New York Times* in **1921** reported that a woman blamed a Ouija board for telling her to leave her mother's **dead body** in the **living room** for **15 days** before burying her in the backyard.

In 1958, Mrs Helen Dow Peck left an amazing **$152,000** in her will to a Mr John Gale Forbes – a **spirit** who had contacted her via her Ouija board!

RETURN OF
THE DEAD

People all over the world believe that there is a night once a year when **ghosts** leave their graves and **wander the earth**.

In Britain and America, this night is **Hallowe'en**, celebrated on **October 31st**. It dates back 2000 years to the Celts in Britain, who believed that the date marked the beginning of darkness and cold. They built **bonfires** to frighten away the spirits, and **feasted** and **danced** around the fires.

Today we light candles in **jack-o'-lanterns** (carved pumpkins) – originally, this was for **protection** against ghosts and witches.

Jack-o'-lanterns are named after an Irish farmer, Stingy Jack, who tried to **trick the Devil**. As a **punishment**, he was cursed to wander the Earth forever, using a candle inside a hollowed-out turnip to **light his way**.

In the **Middle Ages** in the **UK**, beggars would call at all the big houses on Hallowe'en. In return for **food**, they would **pray** that the souls of the dead didn't come back to **haunt** the rich. It was an early version of today's **trick-or-treating**.

Different cultures have different ways of **celebrating** the return of the dead – and it is nearly always a **happy event** to remember dead family and friends.

In **Japan**, a three-day festival is held every summer. People visit their ancestors' graves and light fires to draw the ghosts to the **celebrations**. Afterwards, **floating lanterns** are dropped into rivers or the sea to guide the ghosts back to the spirit world.

China celebrates a **Hungry Ghost Festival**, also in the summer. People leave out food, and put on shows to **entertain** the ghosts. The front row is always **reserved for the dead,** so it remains **empty**. Or does it . . . ?

Like the UK and America, **Mexico** celebrates the **Day of the Dead** on October 31st – it's a festival where people honour the dead with offerings of colourful **sugar skeletons**.

Austrians are much more **serious** on October 31st, which they call **All Saints Day** – they don't have parties, but welcome the dead by leaving **bread**, **water** and a **lighted lamp** on the table before they go to bed.

In **Czechoslovakia**, on November 2nd, people **decorate graves** with flowers and glowing candles, and they put **chairs** around the fireplace – one for every living person in the family, and **one for all the family ghosts**.

On **Hallowe'en** night in **Germany**, October 31st, there's a **spooky superstition** – people put all their **knives** away so that when the spirits return, nobody can get harmed.

The people of **Sumpango** in **Guatemala** have their **Day of the Dead** celebration on November 1st. They climb to the **highest hill** in the town, release colourful **kites** into the sky, and watch as the wind **rips them apart**.

FAKES
EXPOSED

No one has ever been able to **prove** ghosts exist – or that they **definitely don't**. But one thing's for certain: many people involved with the paranormal over the years have been exposed as **fakes**.

In the late **nineteenth century**, when **cameras** were still very new, photos of ghosts were often just a **trick** called '**double exposure**'. Two photographs were taken on top of each other, one of a person and one of an empty room, which made the people in the photo **look like ghosts**. Today fake photos of ghosts can easily be created with **computer programmes**.

Ectoplasm was photographed coming from the **mouths and noses** of Victorian mediums. But it was later discovered that most ectoplasm was **fake**. Mediums chewed up **paper**, **goose fat**, and **egg white** and spat it out to fool people.

Helen Duncan, a **Scottish** medium practising in the early **twentieth century**, was the last person to be **imprisoned** under the **1735 Witchcraft Act**. She was revealed to have eaten thin cloth, then **spewed** it back out, tricking lots of people who had paid to see her **talk to ghosts**.

In the **Berkshire** village of Bucklebury, people were scared by **four ghostly white figures** carrying a **coffin** along country lanes at night . . . Until one evening a brave man lay in wait, jumped out at the ghosts and **beat** them with a **stick**. He soon realised that they were **just men** – and when they ran away, dropping the 'coffin', it turned out to be a **stolen sheep**!

In the **1930s**, the Irving family on the **Isle of Man** claimed to share their farmhouse with **Gef the Talking Mongoose**, never seen but often heard. Gef told them he was "an extra extra clever mongoose". Psychic investigators visited the farm and found **no proof** – instead they suspected that the daughter was a **ventriloquist**.

Throughout the late nineteenth century, **Borley Rectory** was believed to be the most haunted house in England – then it turned out that the Reverend Henry Bull had **faked hauntings** to attract visitors and make money. The **ghostly** playing of the 'magic piano' was in fact his six-year-old **plucking the piano strings with a poker** from the back.

In **1762**, crowds of **Londoners** paid to visit the house of Richard Parsons for the chance of hearing the **Cock Lane Ghost**. Mr Parsons said the ghost communicated by knocking once for yes and twice for no. But when his daughter, Betty, was found in bed with a wooden board she'd been using to create the ghost's knocks, the **hoax** was exposed – and the ghost was never heard again.

PARANORMAL
PUZZLES

While some supernatural stories turn out to be fakes, there are many **tantalising tales** left **unexplained**.

At the **Bow Bells** pub in **London**, the **ladies' loos** sometimes flush all by themselves when someone is sitting on them. Could it be a **mischievous** ghost – or just a case of **dodgy plumbing**?

Cleopatra's Needle, which stands on the Embankment, **London**, was a gift from Egypt in **1819**. It wasn't easy to transport, and several sailors were **drowned** during the journey. Could that be why a **ghostly naked man** is often said to be seen dashing from behind the monument and jumping into the Thames **without a splash**?

Is there any truth in the legend of the **Screaming Skull**? In the **sixteenth century**, Burton Agnes Hall was built in **Yorkshire** for three sisters. One of the sisters was **stabbed** to death, and as she was dying she asked her sisters to **remove her head** and keep it in the house for ever. Her sisters didn't keep their promise, and the hall was filled with **strange moaning** until her skull was finally returned.

In the mid-nineteenth century, the **attic** room at a boarding house, **50 Berkeley Square, London**, had a reputation for being haunted. A nobleman once stayed as a dare, and was so **terrified he never spoke again**. But **what** did he see?

In **1872**, the **Mary Celeste** was found **abandoned** in the middle of the Atlantic. Its crew of seven had **vanished** into thin air and were **never seen again**. The weather was fine, and the crew were experienced sailors. So **where** did they go?

In **Graceland Cemetery** in the USA, there's a glass case containing the statue of a little girl, Inez Clarke, who was **struck by lightning** in the **late 1800s**. Legend claims that when there's a storm, the glass case is found **empty**. People have even said that if you listen quietly, you can hear the sound of a girl **crying**.

In the **1800s**, a rich man bought a mummy in **Egypt**, then walked away into the desert, **never to be seen again**. The mummy was displayed at the **British Museum in London**, and everyone who came into contact with it was said to suffer **misfortune** and sometimes even death. According to legend, the museum kept the case and sold the '**unlucky mummy**' to an American collector. But that wasn't the end of the story . . .

In **April 1912**, the mummy was **secretly** taken aboard a passenger liner to **America**. It never arrived. The liner **struck an iceberg** and **sank**, taking the mummy and **1,517** passengers and crew with it. The liner was none other than the most **famous** shipwreck in history: the **Titanic**. **No trace** of the mummy has **ever** been found.

Bye!

HORRID HENRY BOOKS

Visit Horrid Henry's website at **www.horridhenry.co.uk**
for competitions, games, downloads and a monthly newsletter.

the
orion star

★ ★ ★